BIBLE STORIES

ACTIVITY BOOK
FOR KIDS

This Book
Belongs To:

_____

_____

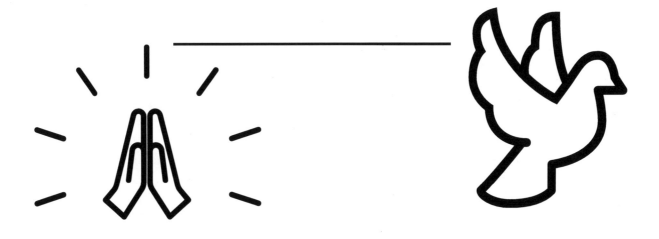

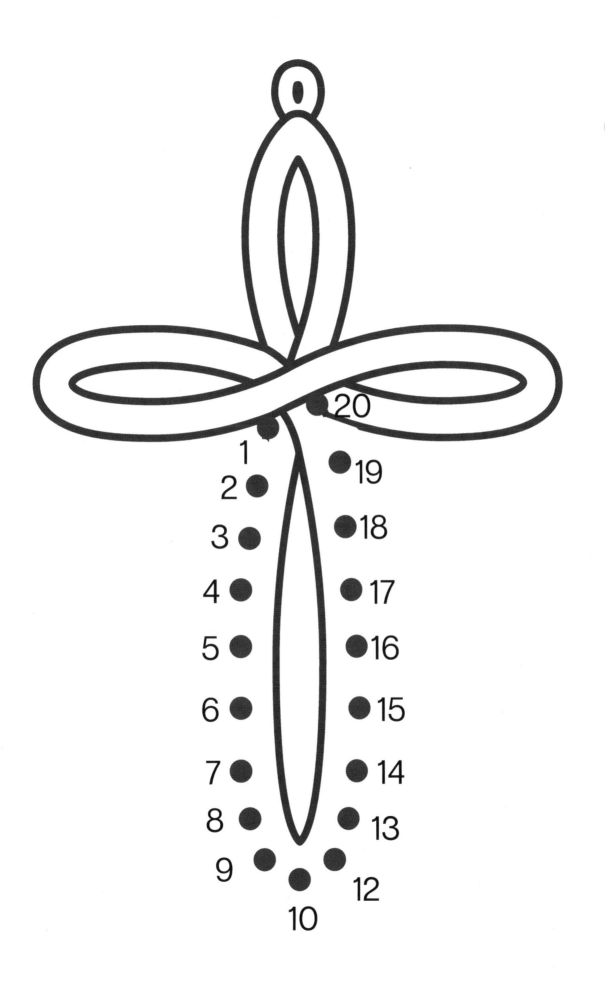

Help the whale through the maze.

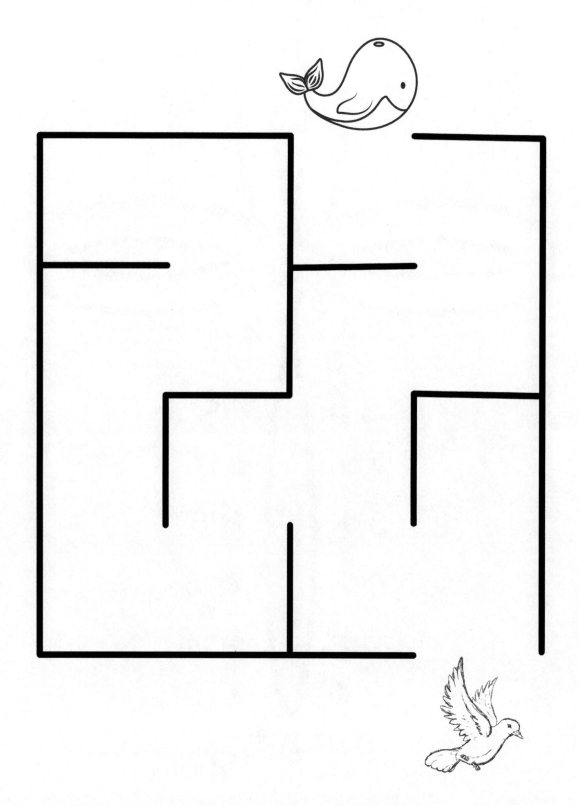

Word Search

Circle The Words Below

```
B A E L T S O P A
N R O O P K G S T
A C F M M E R E O
D H T Y V I S L N
T A L T E R R D E
R R A A O S U D M
F Y L W E R S A E
I U L U L E P S N
N H D A D V E N T
```

advent   apostle

alter   atonement

Count And Trace

1

2

Spot The Difference

Count And Trace

1

2

3

4

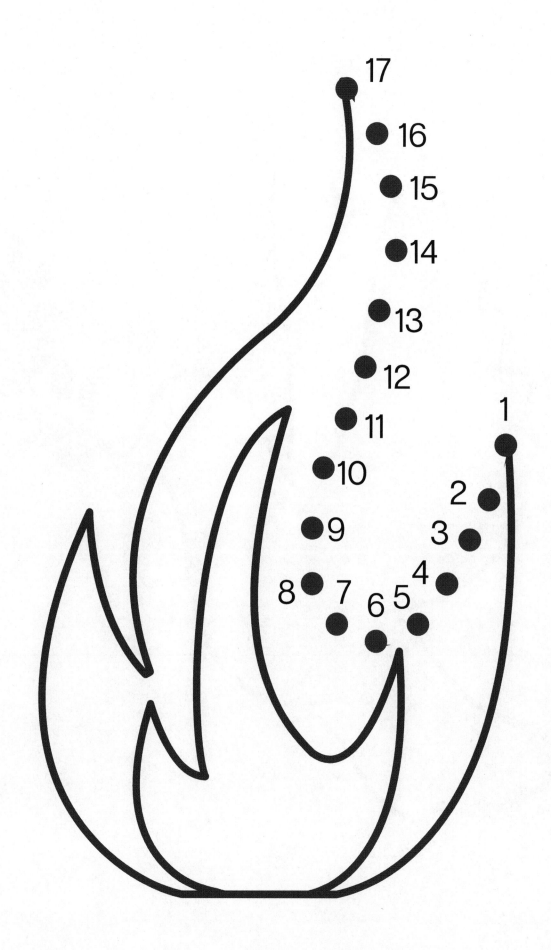

Help the flaming bush through the maze.

Word Search

Circle The Words Below

```
D U D N C L U R T
E A Q O S D K C B
H P N W C R M R C
T I A D R S Y A H
O O X I I G A N E
R C A T B L K E R
T R P B F N S W U
E A R V L E T G B
B R E T H R E N E
```

baptism   brethren

betrothed   cherub

Count And Trace

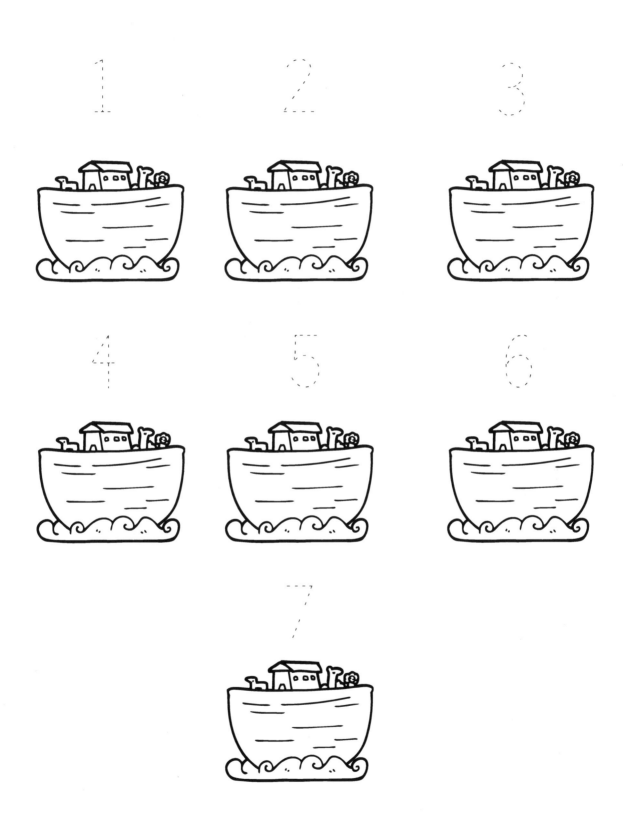

Spot The Difference

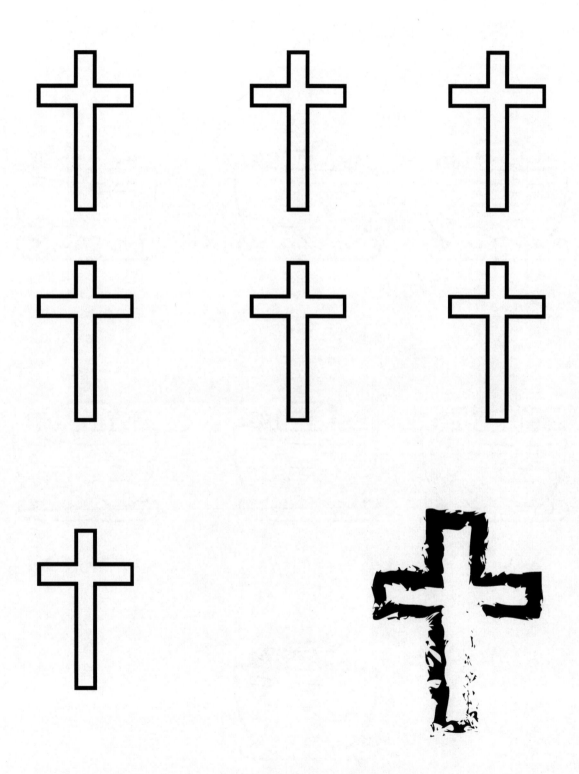

Count And Trace

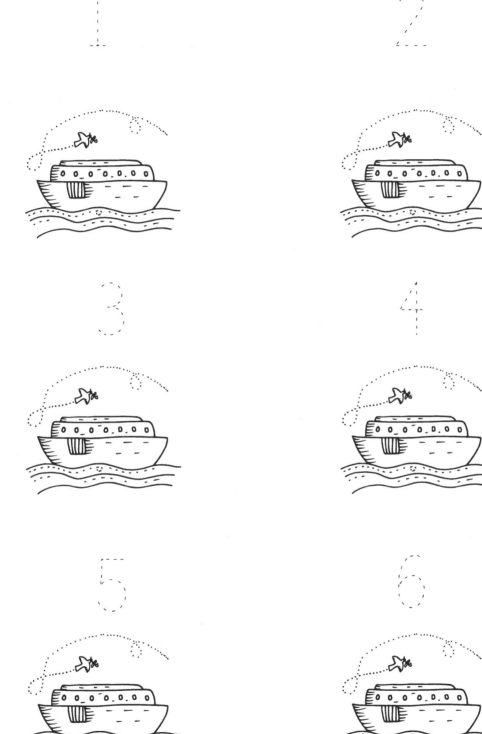

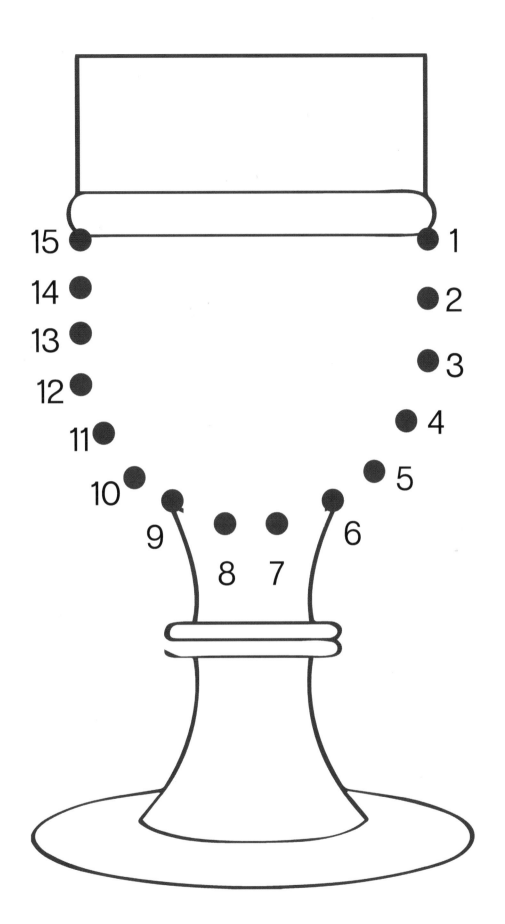

Help the bible through the maze.

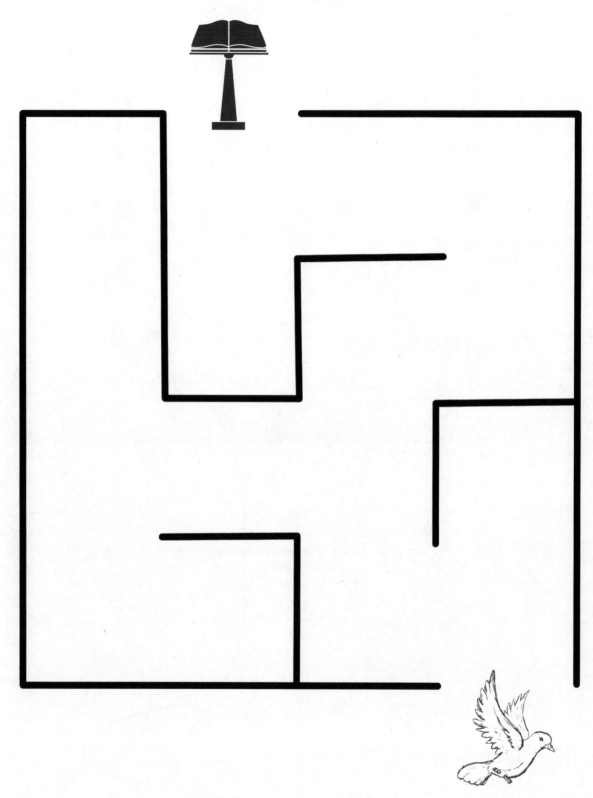

Word Search

Circle The Words Below

```
C Y N A H P I P E
J D L N R F I X H
S I E L A D O E O
G S N C D D H A C
R C E Y U E D L K
A I E S V T L R E
S P N R I I S H Y
S L A H N L O E M
F E L B I L L A F
```

disciple   exodus

epiphany   fallible

Count And Trace

1

2

3

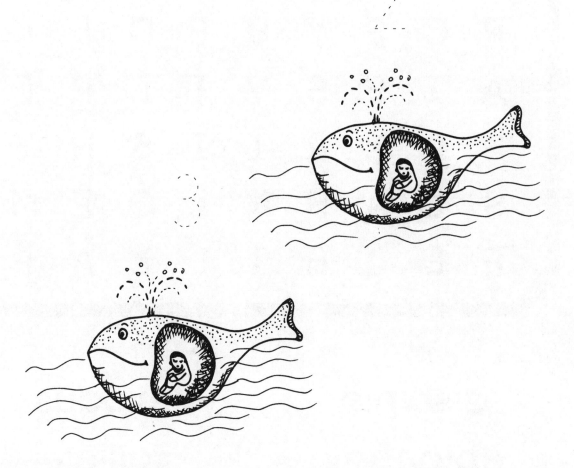

Spot The Differences

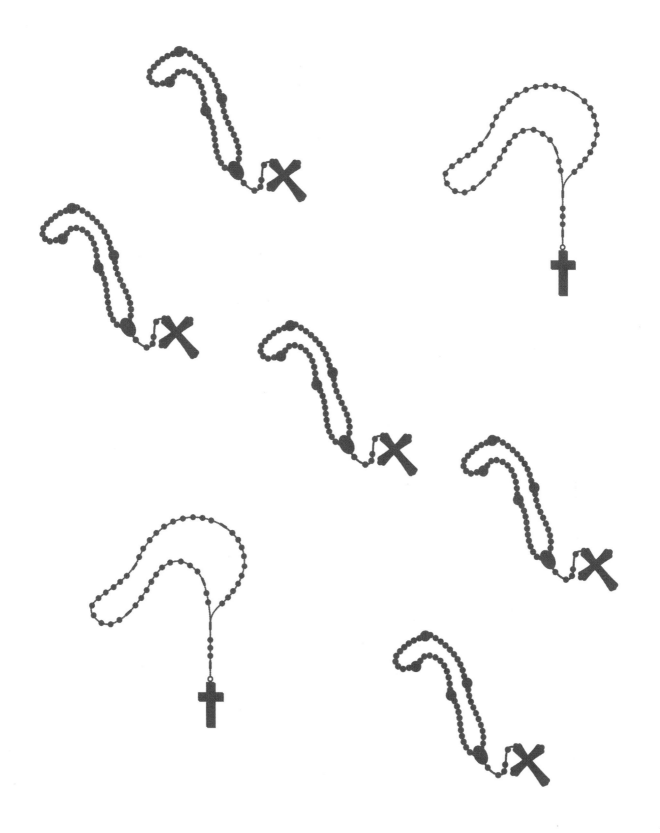

Count And Trace

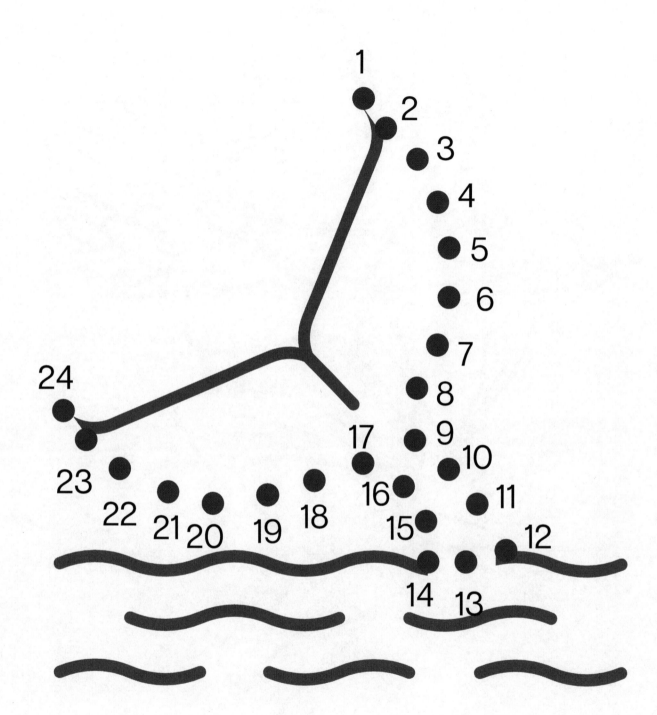

Help moses
through the maze.

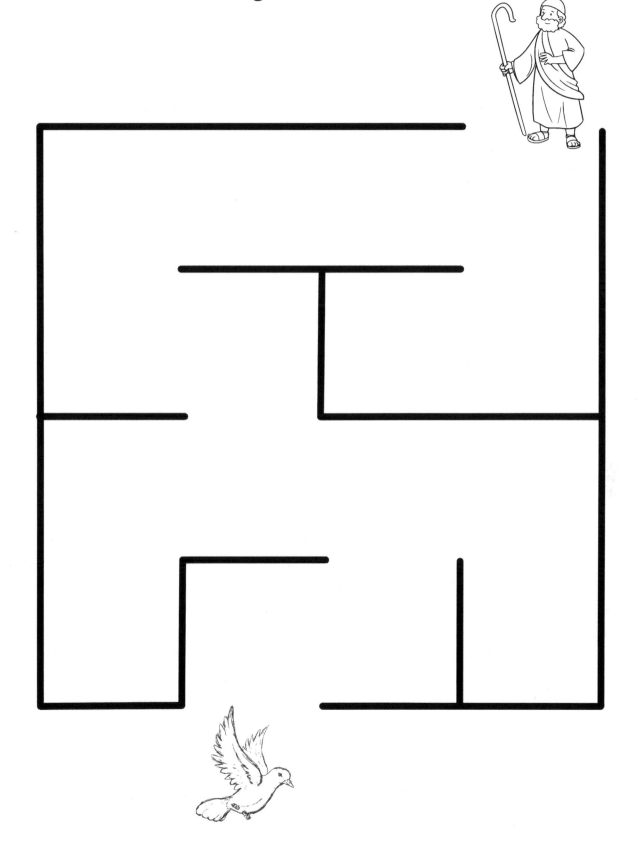

Word Search

Circle The Words Below

```
H A N D B A L L B
B A X O R L I Y I
F N G E U E N R S
L E O L E O T T O
Y V L T T A J A N
A A F T R R U L W
R E U A R O D O E
K L K C R W O D R
G E S N E C N I U
```

gluttony   incense

idolatry   leaven

Count And Trace

Spot The Difference

Count And Trace

1

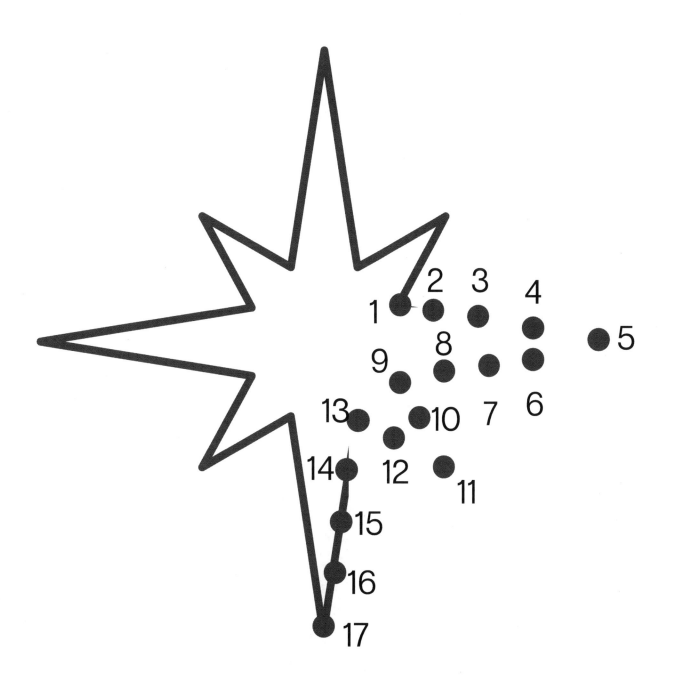

Help adam and eve through the maze.

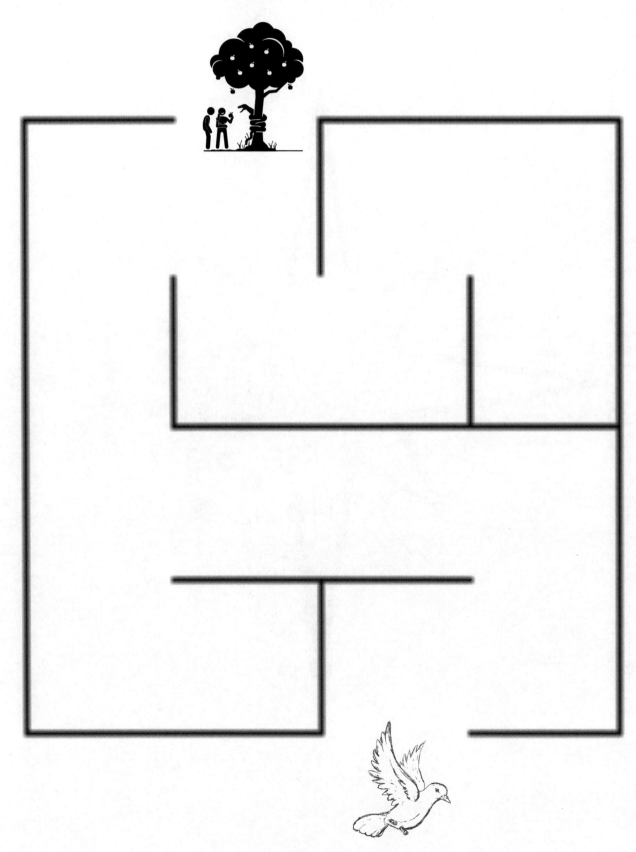

Word Search

Circle The Words Below

```
P A R A B L E E L
A A F S P H E E O
R L A S S A V A C
A O A G I I E R H
D O E R A S R L R
I P P T B S F O O
S X H N I E W W A
E A T U N M P O C
N A R S A A G E R
```

leviathan   parable

messiah   paradise

Count And Trace

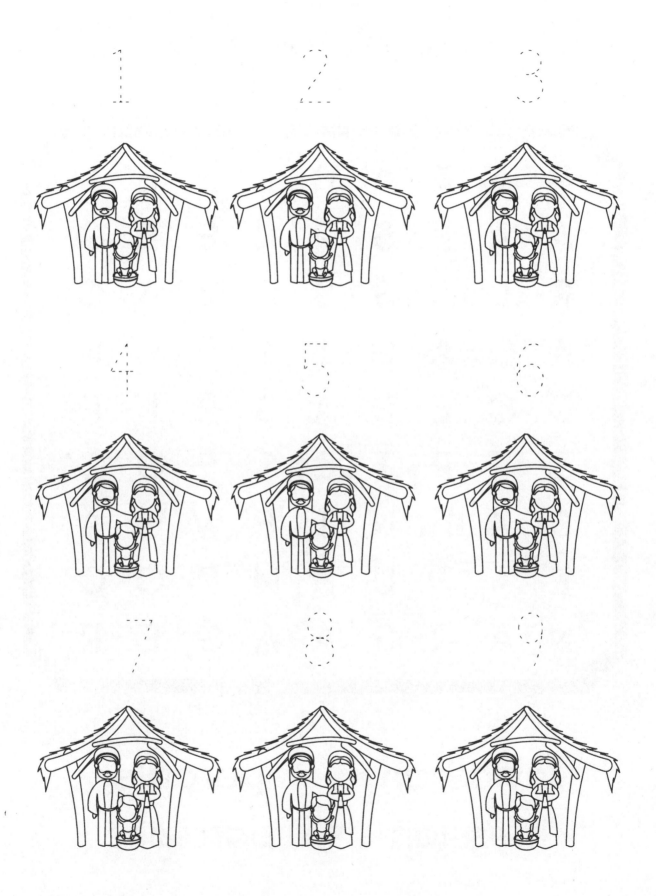

Spot The Difference

Count And Trace

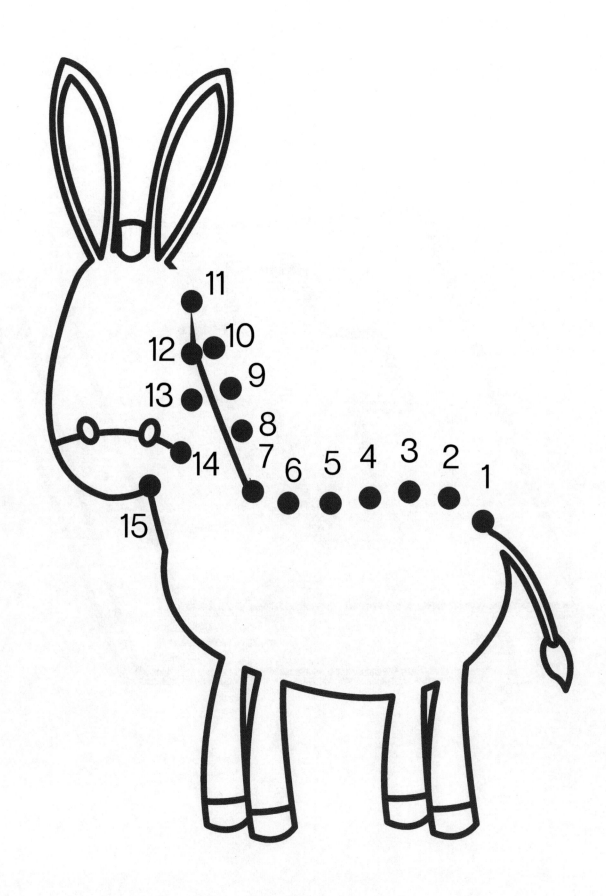

Help mary through the maze.

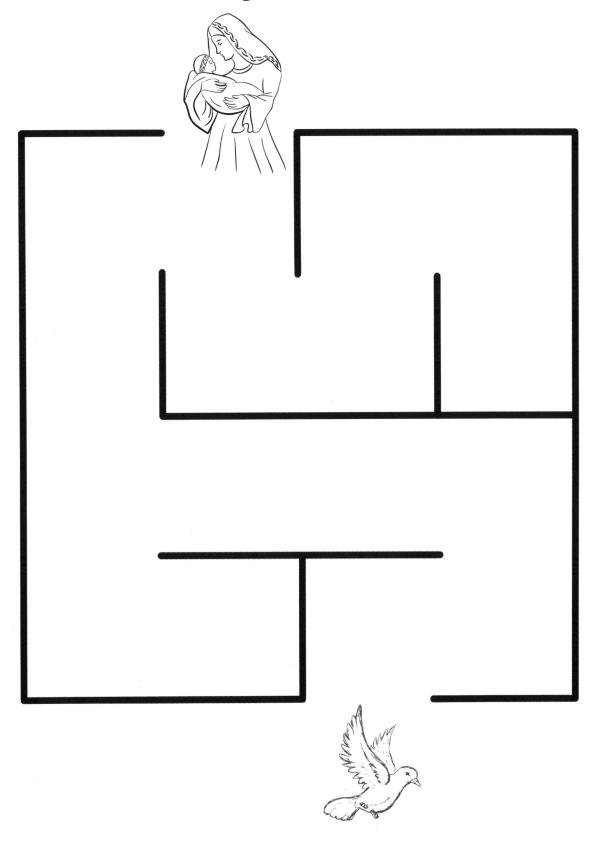

Word Search

Circle The Words Below

```
H  E  G  N  I  F  R  U  S
R  C  A  N  O  O  N  D  W
E  T  R  E  H  O  Y  I  I
S  E  A  A  S  T  R  Y  N
S  N  R  E  I  B  E  B  O
A  N  A  E  R  R  R  O  D
G  I  H  E  E  L  T  L  R
E  S  N  A  P  L  S  A  A
T  L  A  G  I  D  O  R  P
```

pardon   perish

patriarch   prodigal

COUNT AND TRACE

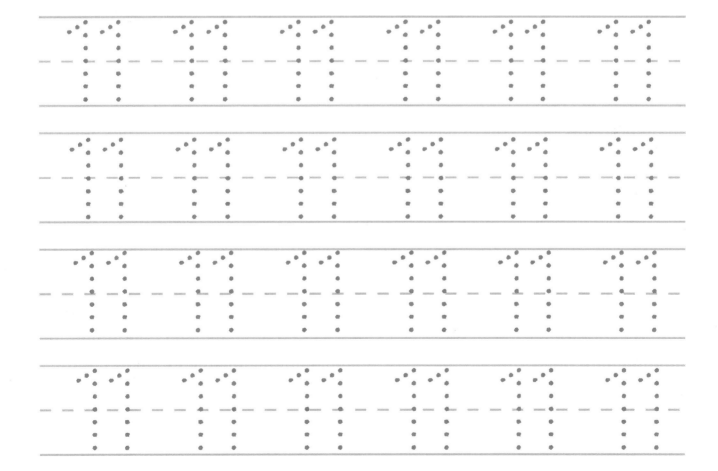

Spot The Difference

COUNT AND TRACE

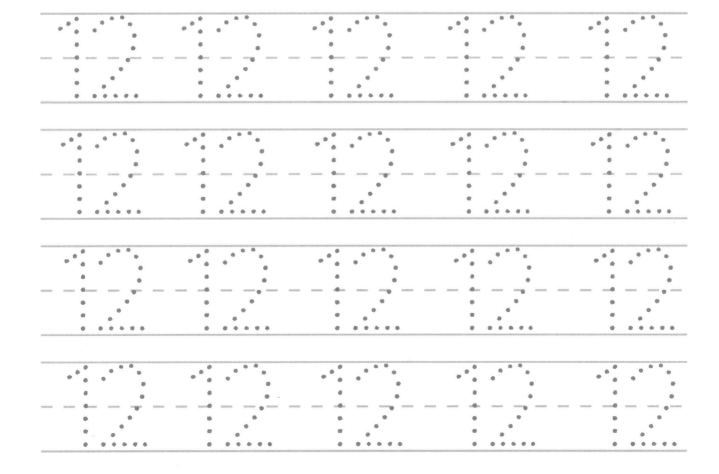

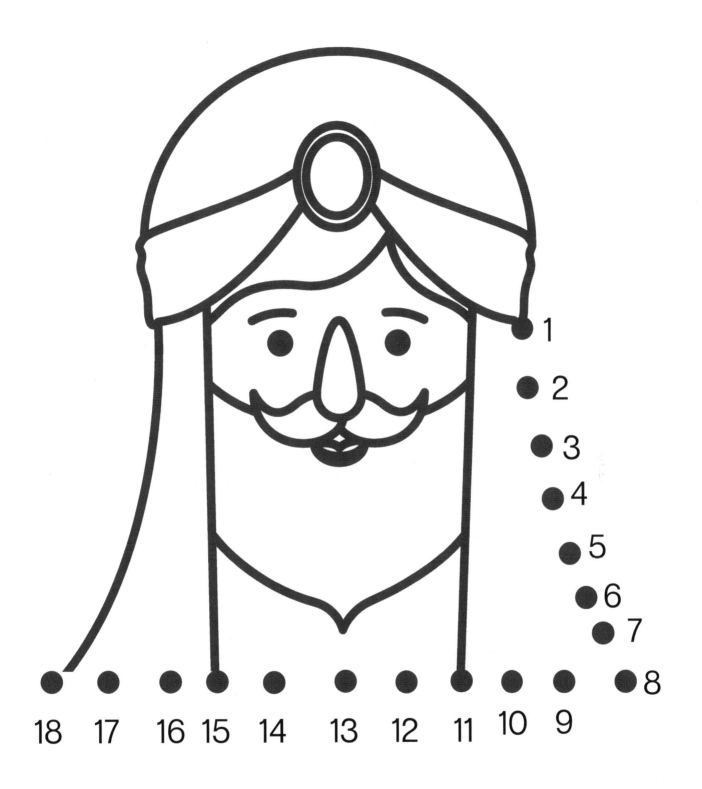

1
2
3
4
5
6
7
8
18 17 16 15 14 13 12 11 10 9

Help the cross through the maze.

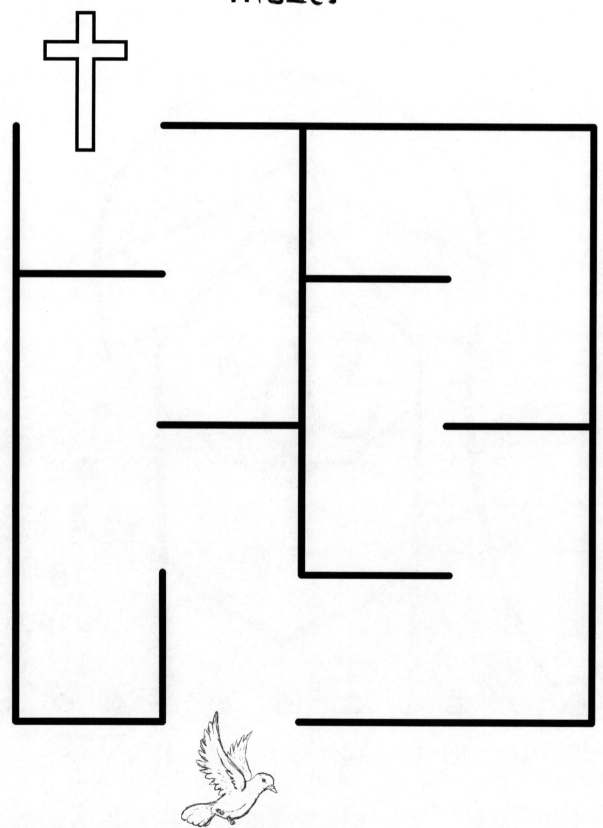

Word Search

Circle The Words Below

```
P R O P H E T E B
O R E J O I C E U
G A O T B E E T T
I P N P D E L N T
R T A R H V D B E
T U O S C E R P R
H R N F A L C O F
G E A N R S T Y L
T R I A T H L O N
```

prophecy   rapture

prophet   rejoice

COUNT AND TRACE

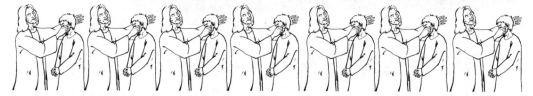

13

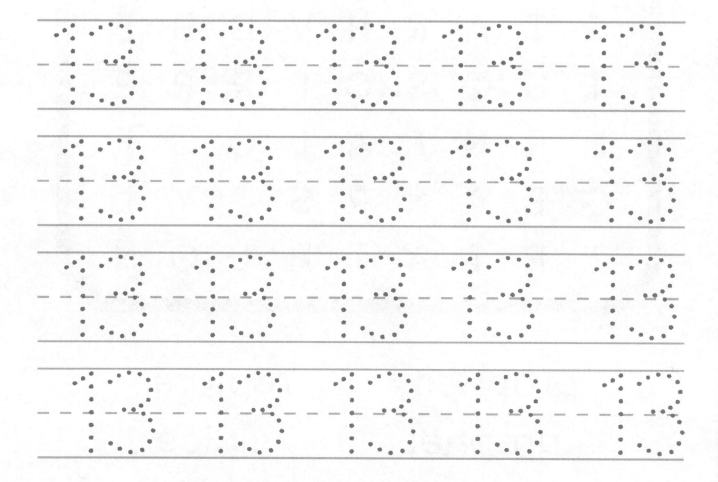

Spot The Differences

COUNT AND TRACE

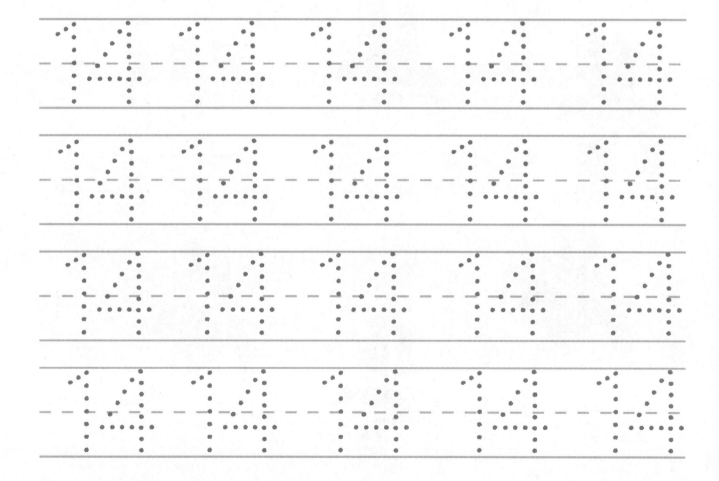

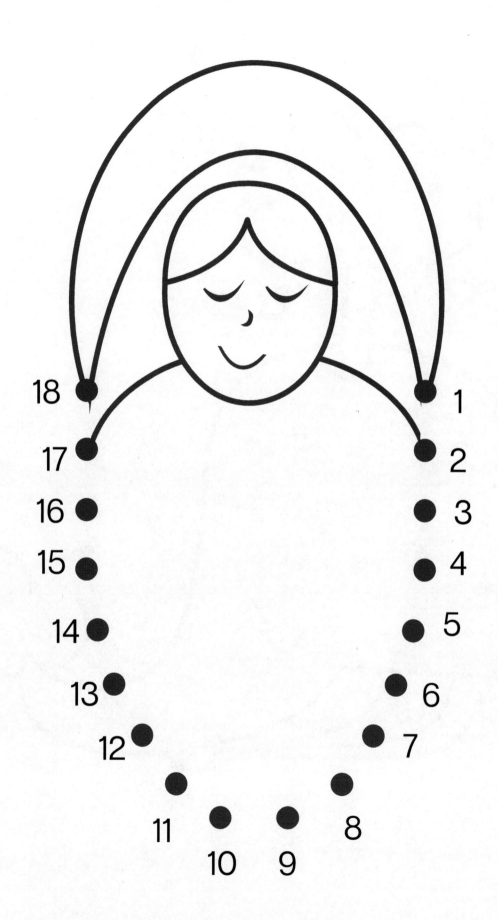

18   1

17   2

16   3

15   4

14   5

13   6

12   7

11   8

10   9

Help the ark through the maze.

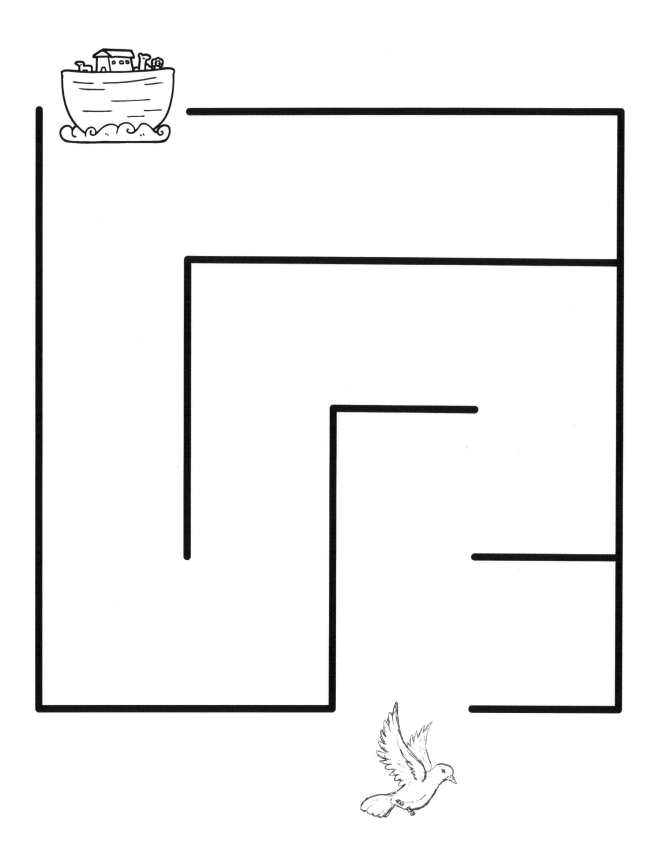

Word Search

Circle The Words Below

```
N O M R E S S R D
R U T I N A R H T
E U U H C C D E
S I G T E R M A K
T F A B R I S S C
L R P S Y F I W I
W H P U R I N M R
N U M I D C T A C
R I G H T E O U S
```

righteous   sermon

sacrifice   wrath

COUNT AND TRACE

15

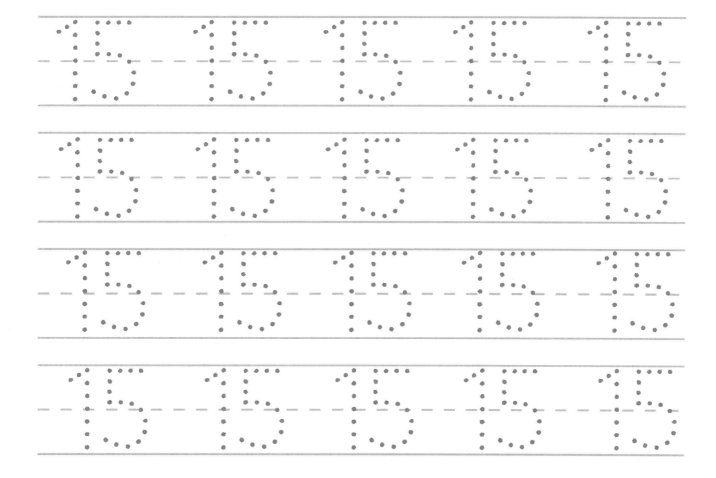

Spot The Difference

COUNT AND TRACE

16

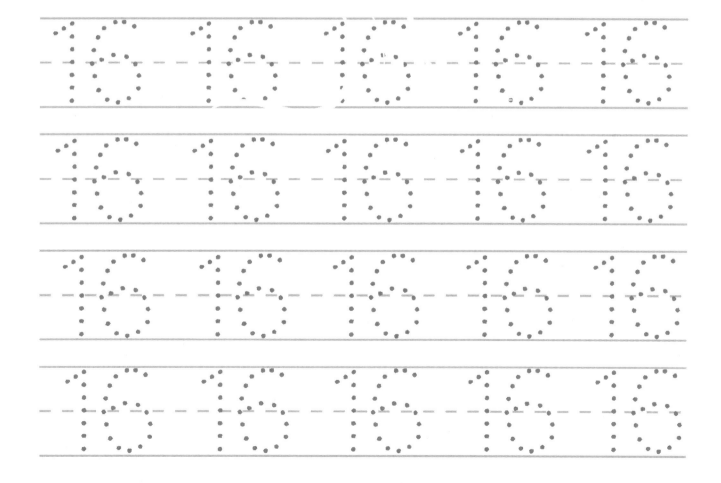

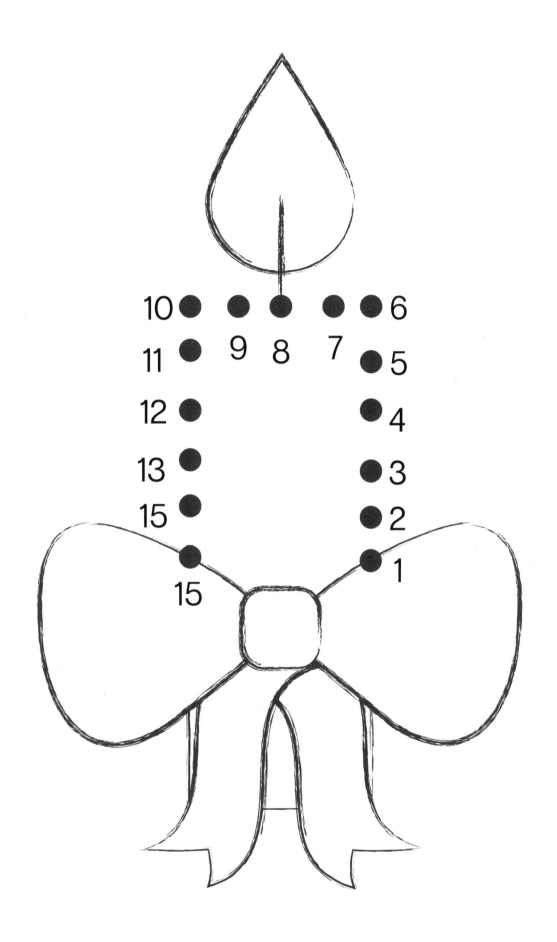

Help the bird through the maze.

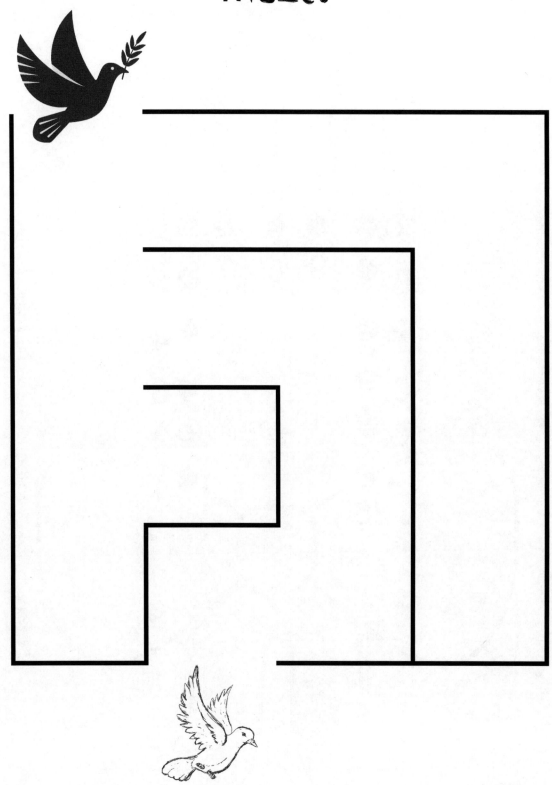

Word Search

Circle The Words Below

```
L U I N L K R A M
B A T S I D S C A
O C C A G I A R T
A A O R S R C E T
T N U E O M F E H
I O N E N L U K E
N E N R I T S I W
G N I X O B H E R
L D Y C G T A N E
```

genesis   mark

matthew   luke

COUNT AND TRACE

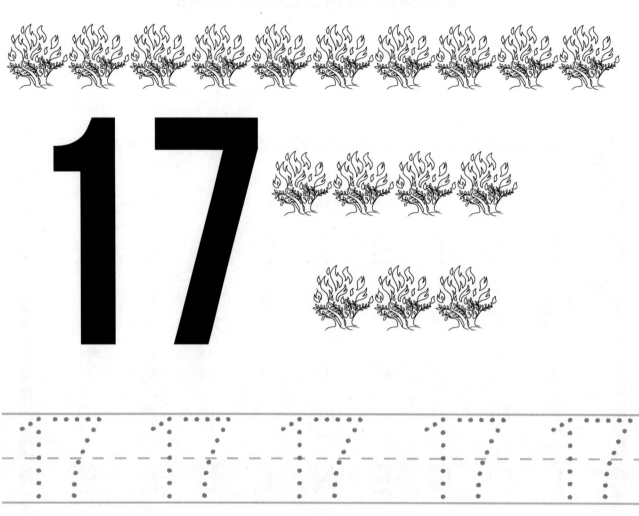

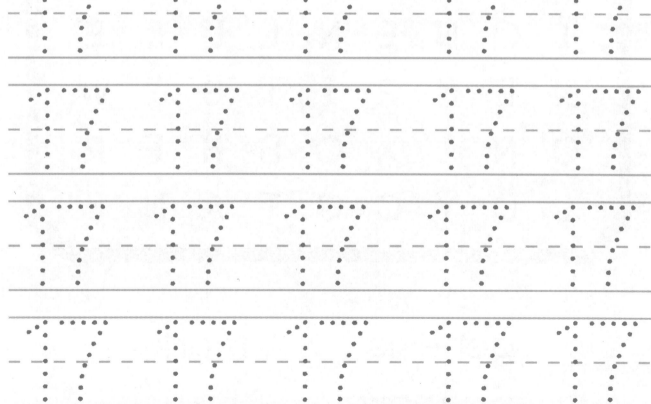

Spot The Differences

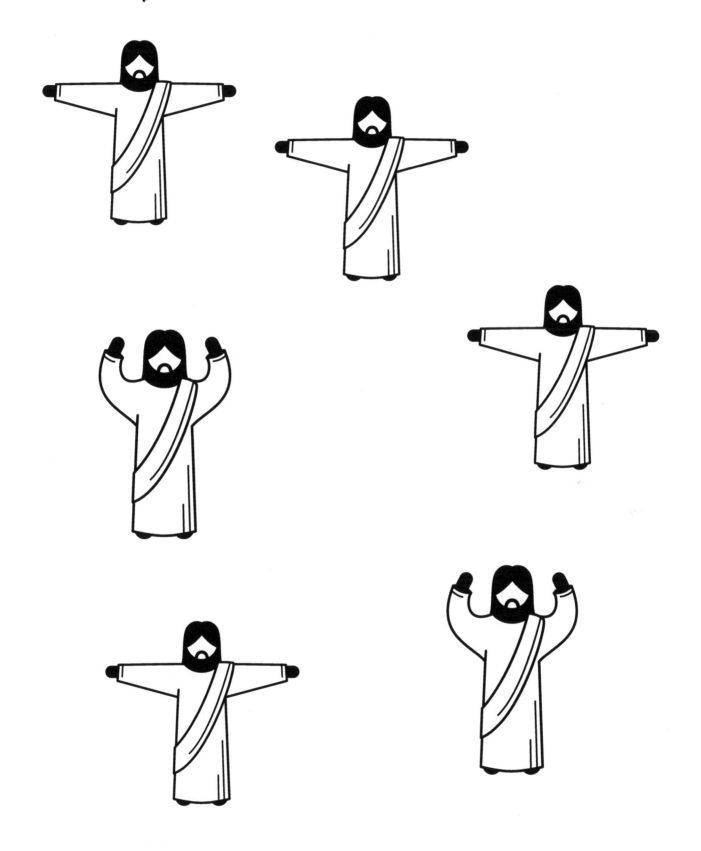

COUNT AND TRACE

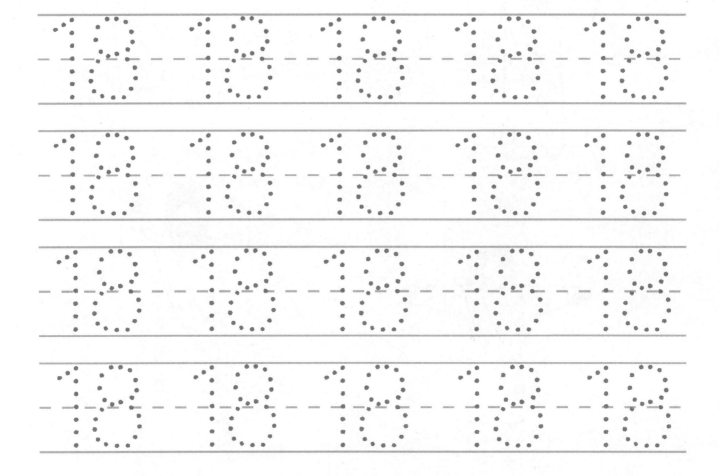

Help mary through the maze.

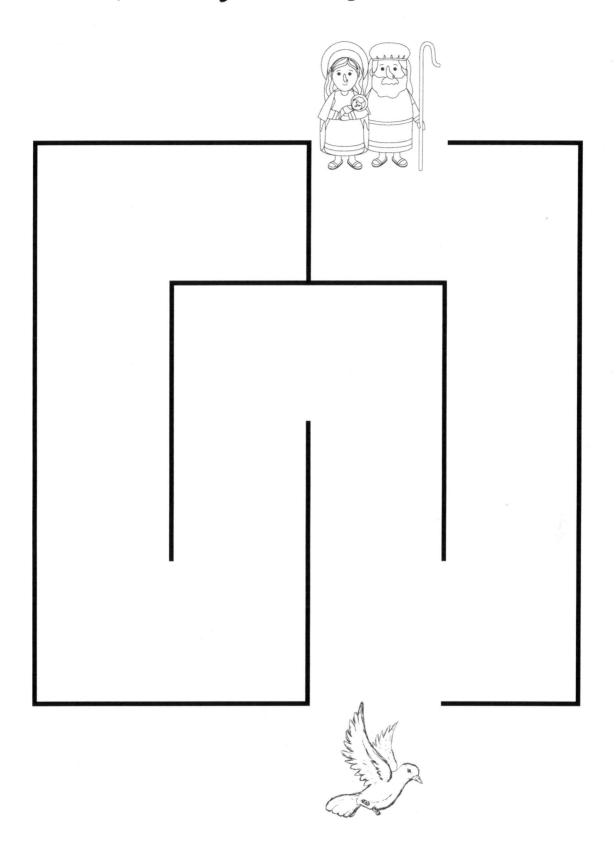

Word Search

Circle The Words Below

```
G  S  K  R  A  P  A  P  A  R  P
A  A  F  O  P  I  E  S  A  L
L  N  I  F  R  U  J  S  D
A  L  I  E  O  G  O  A  D
T  I  T  U  S  I  H  I  O
I  F  T  I  S  C  N  D  C
A  I  D  X  E  A  N  W  K
N  I  E  U  G  A  T  T  I
S  N  A  M  O  R  T  S  E
```

john   titus

romans   galatians

COUNT AND TRACE

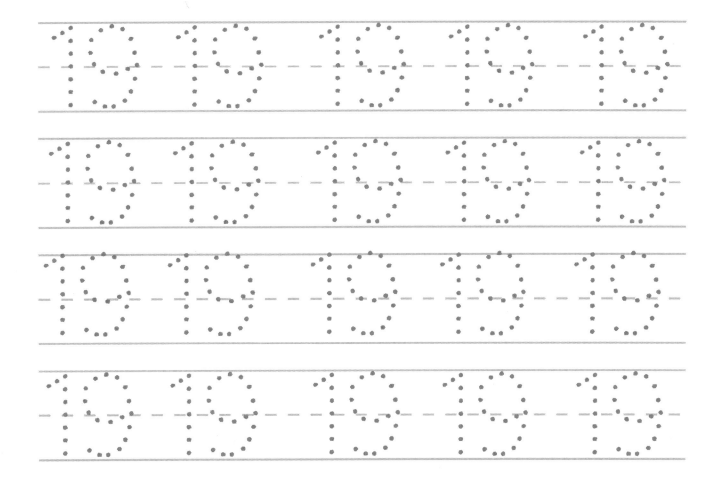

Spot The Differences

COUNT AND TRACE

20

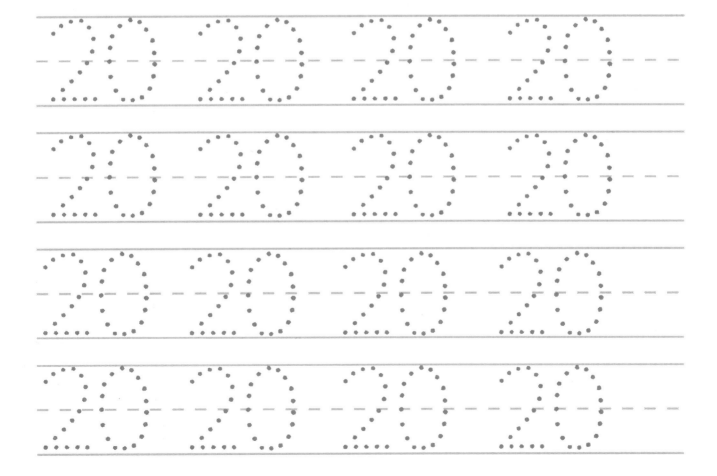

Help the whale
through the maze.

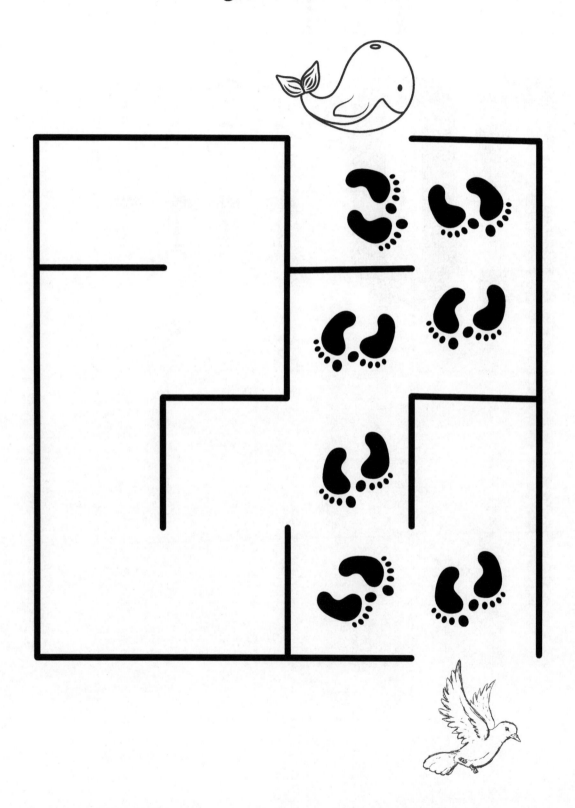

Word Search

Circle The Words Below

```
B A E L T S O P A
N R O O P K G S T
A C F M M E R E O
D H T Y V I S L N
T A L T E R R D E
R R A A O S U D M
F Y L W E R S A E
I U L U L E P S N
N H D A D V E N T
```

advent   apostle

alter   atonement

Spot The Difference

Help the flaming bush through the maze.

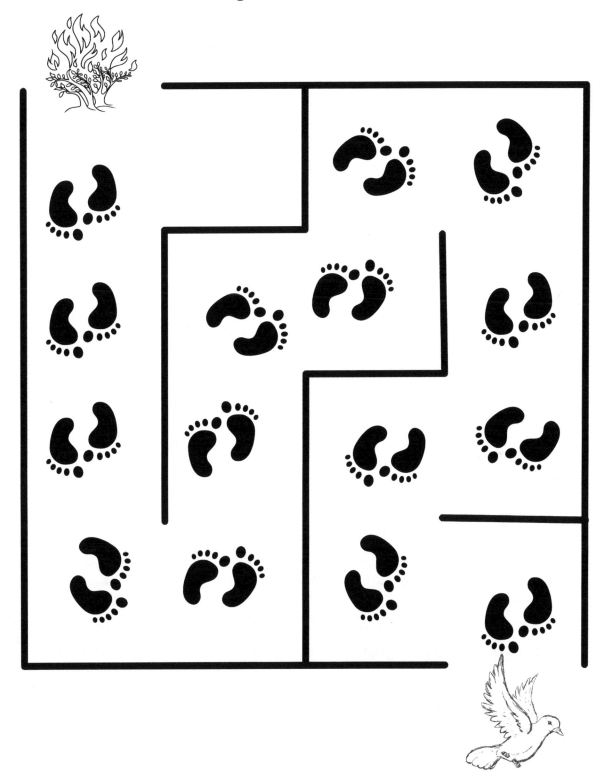

Word Search

Circle The Words Below

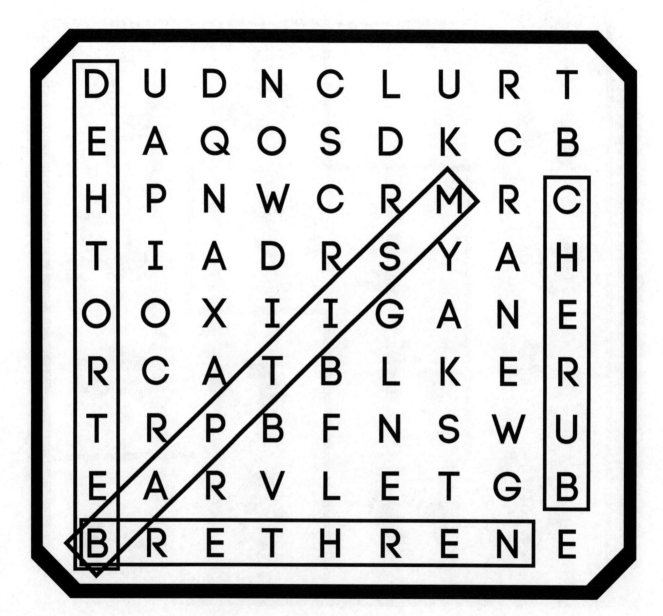

baptism   brethren

betrothed   cherub

Spot The Difference

Help the bible through the maze.

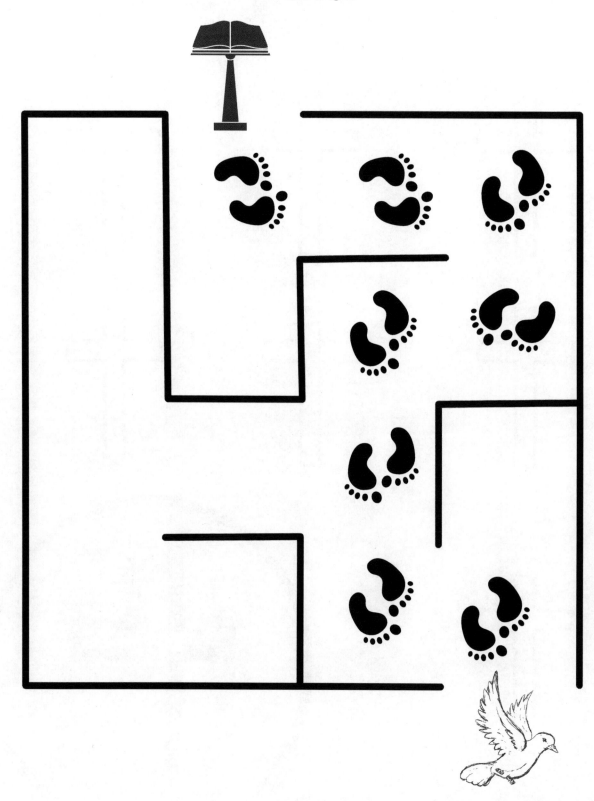

Word Search

Circle The Words Below

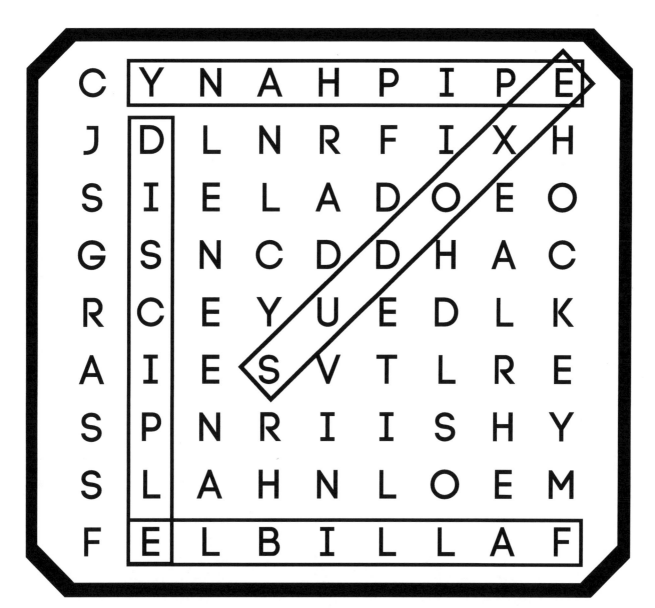

```
C Y N A H P I P E
J D L N R F I X H
S I E L A D O E O
G S N C D D H A C
R C E Y U E D L K
A I E S V T L R E
S P N R I I S H Y
S L A H N L O E M
F E L B I L L A F
```

disciple   exodus

epiphany   fallible

Spot The Differences

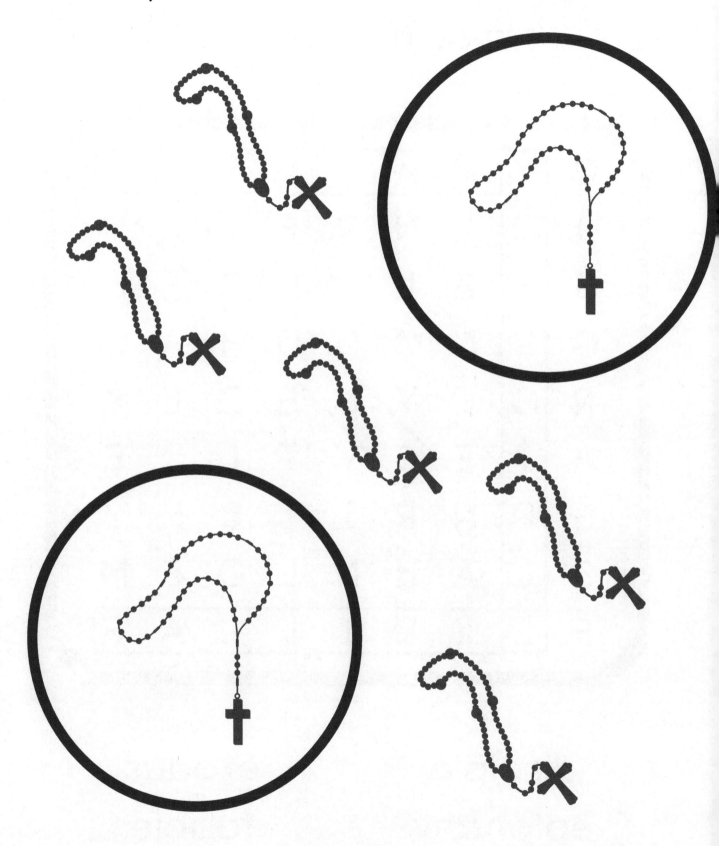

Help moses
through the maze.

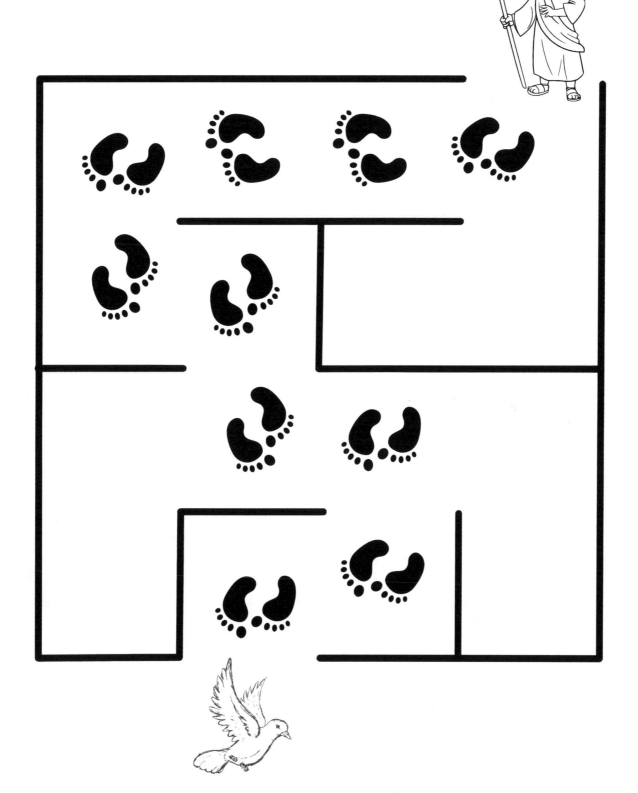

Word Search

Circle The Words Below

```
H A N D B A L L B B
B A X O R L I Y I
F N G E U E N R S
L E O L E O T T O
Y V L T T A J A N
A A F T R R U L W
R E U A R O D O E
K L K C R W O D R
G E S N E C N I U
```

gluttony   incense

idolatry   leaven

Spot The Difference

Help adam and eve through the maze.

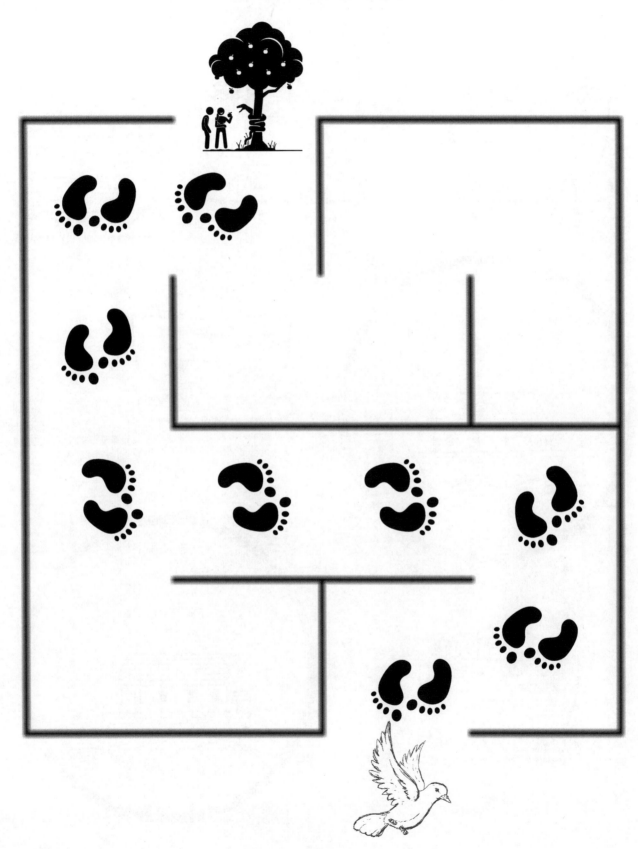

Word Search

Circle The Words Below

```
P A R A B L E E L E L
A A F S P H E E O
R L A S S A V A C
A O A G I I E R H
D O E R A S R L R
I P P T B S F O O
S X H N I E W W A
E A T U N M P O C
N A R S A A G E R
```

leviathan   parable

messiah   paradise

Spot The Difference

Help mary
through the maze.

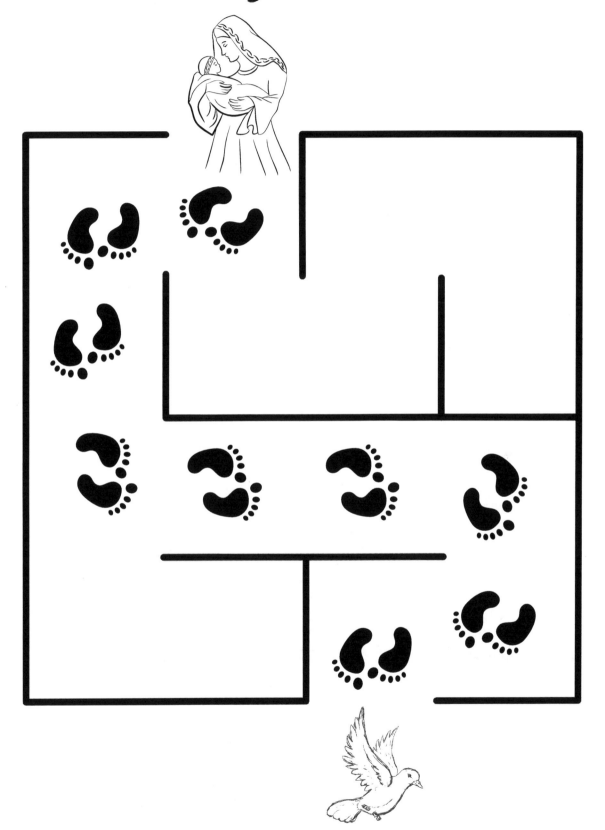

Word Search

Circle The Words Below

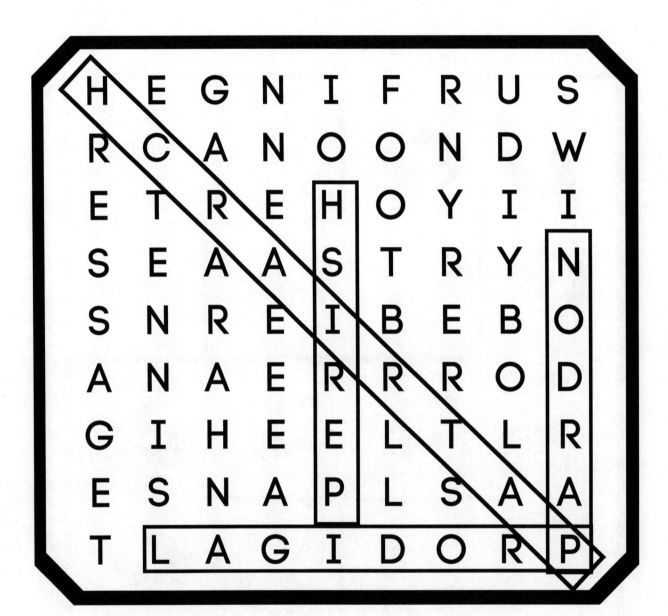

```
H E G N I F R U S
R C A N O O N D W
E T R E H O Y I I
S E A A S T R Y N
S N R E I B E B O
A N A E R R R O D
G I H E E L T L R
E S N A P L S A A
T L A G I D O R P
```

pardon   perish

patriarch   prodigal

Spot The Difference

Help the cross through the maze.

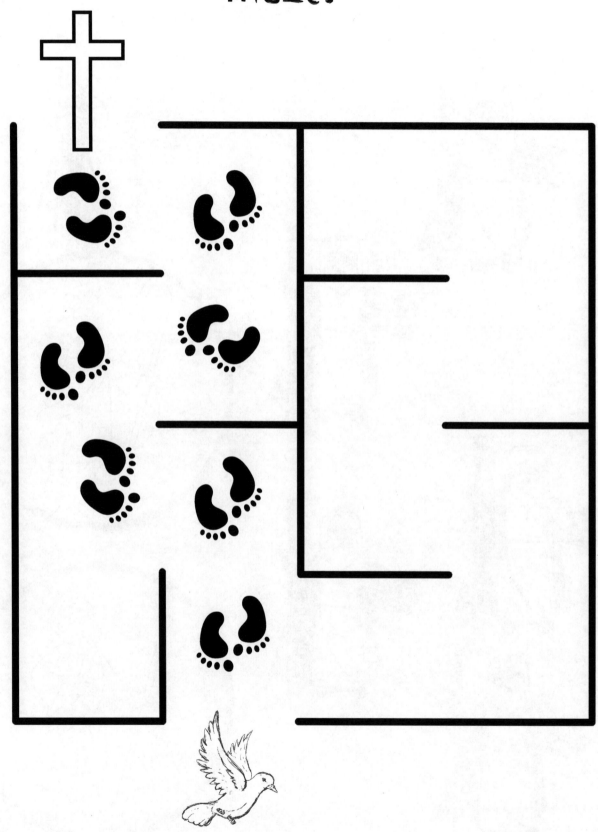

Word Search

Circle The Words Below

```
P R O P H E T E B
O R E J O I C E U
G A O T B E E T T
I P N P D E L N T
R T A R H V D B E
T U O S C E R P R
H R N F A L C O F
G E A N R S T Y L
T R I A T H L O N
```

prophecy   rapture

prophet   rejoice

Spot The Differences

Help the ark through the maze.

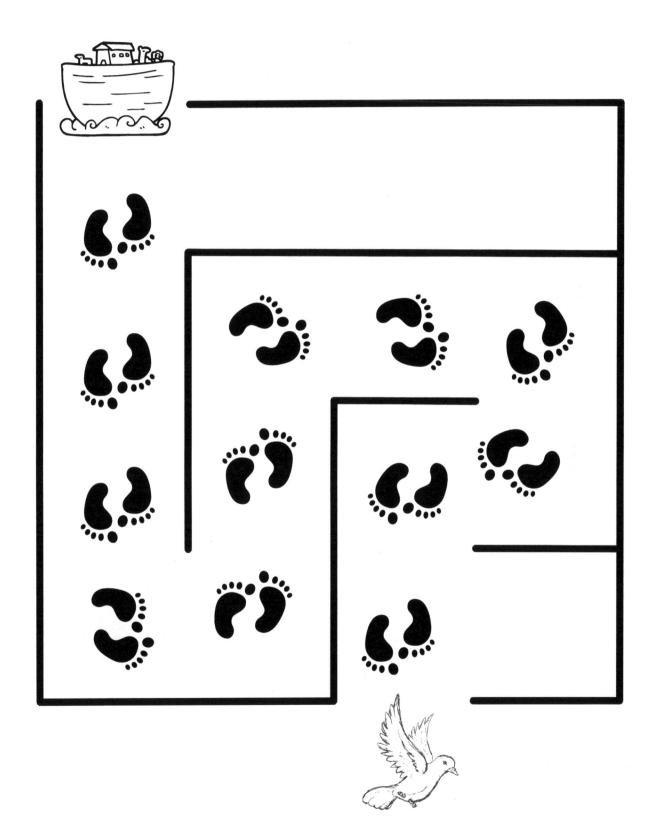

Word Search

Circle The Words Below

```
N O M R E S   S R D
  R U T I N A   R H T
  E U U H C   C D E
  S I G T E R   M A K
  T F A B R I   S S C
  L R P S Y F   I W I
  W H P U R I   N M R
  N U M I D C   T A C
  R I G H T E O U S
```

righteous   sermon

sacrifice   wrath

Spot The Difference

Help the bird through the maze.

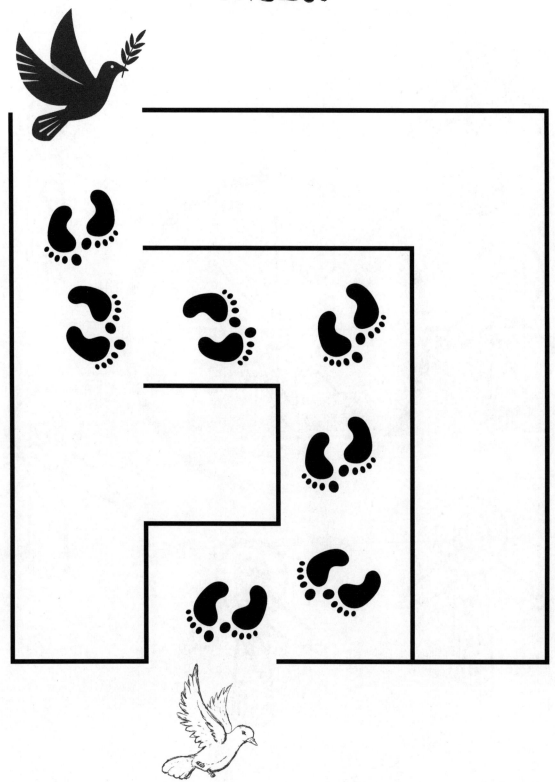

Word Search

Circle The Words Below

```
L U I N L K R A M
B A T S I D S C A
O C C A G I A R T
A A O R S R C E T
T N U E O M F E H
I O N E N L U K E
N E N R I T S I W
G N I X O B H E R
L D Y C G T A N E
```

genesis   mark

matthew   luke

Spot The Differences

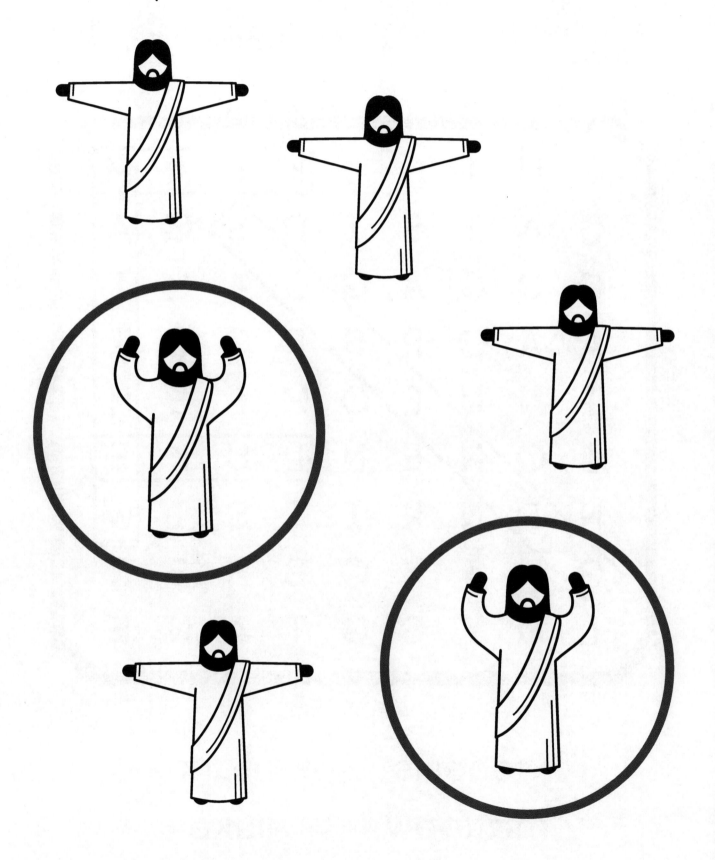

Help mary and joseph through the maze.

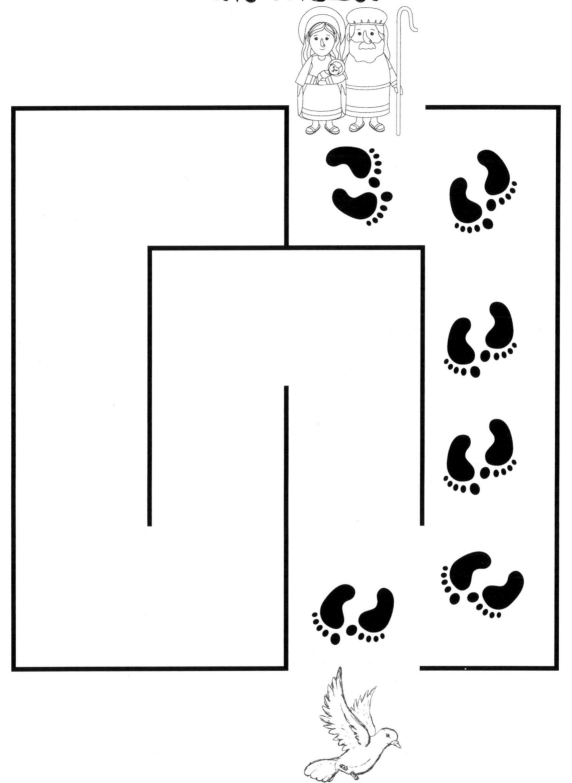

Word Search

Circle The Words Below

```
G  S  K  R  A  P  A  R  P
A  A  F  O  P  I  E  S  A
L  N  I  F  R  U  J  S  D
A  L  I  E  O  G  O  A  D
T  I  T  U  S  I  H  I  O
I  F  T  I  S  C  N  D  C
A  I  D  X  E  A  N  W  K
N  I  E  U  G  A  T  T  I
S  N  A  M  O  R  T  S  E
```

john   titus

romans   galatians

Spot The Differences

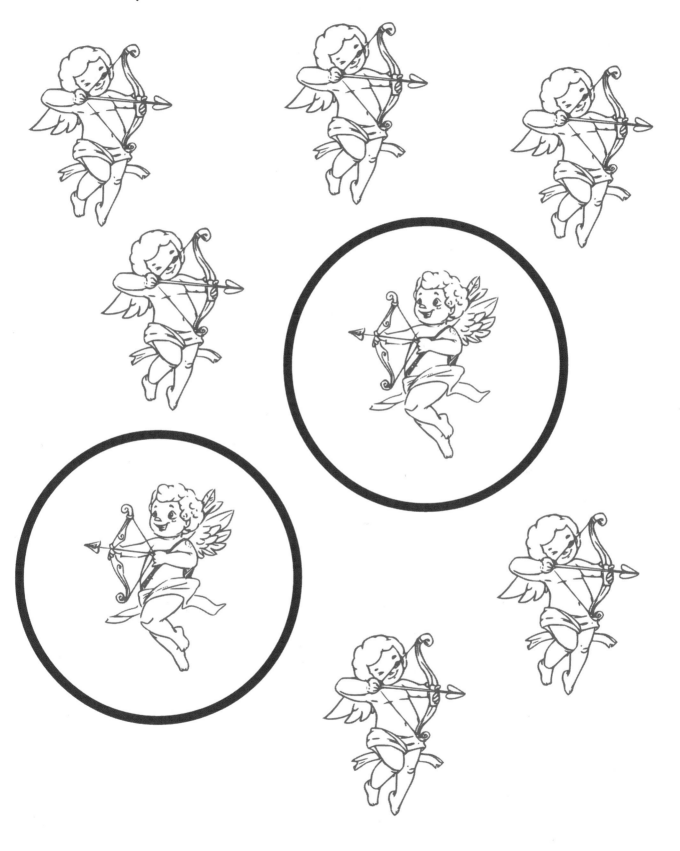

Made in the USA
Columbia, SC
07 January 2025

51379590R00057